New Mags City Guide
Stockholm

For years, I've traveled the world as a design and lifestyle expert. Every time I discover an inspiring place, I make a note of it. Over time, this list has grown to include many outstanding destinations. People often ask me for travel recommendations. Obviously, most people don't have the time to find the best spots, because it requires time, and time is a scarce resource for many. That's why we created this series of city guides. Not just any collection of guides, but the best, most beautiful, and most practical, presented as a real book. I believe the ideal city guide is tangible, something you can bring along on your journey, especially handy when your smartphone runs out of battery.

Special thanks to Jesper Svangaard from New Mags for his enthusiasm and publishing expertise, and to Mario Depicolzuane, our art director, whose studio's design brought this guide to life. I'm also deeply grateful to all the incredible locations featured and to everyone who helped bring this project to life.

We hope that you, as a reader, will embrace our city guide and find it valuable on your travels. After all, that's the true purpose of this book.

TABLE OF CONTENTS

MAXIN

Surrounded by a cluster of islands known as the archipelago, Stockholm reveals its beauty from above, even before you arrive at the Airport. The sea and nature seamlessly weave into the city's structure in the most natural way. In the summer, the city buzzes with life as everyone rushes to the streets and the sea to soak in the sun. In winter, when the snow falls, the city transforms into a fairytale setting. I used to travel to Stockholm in the wintertime for the design and furniture events, hardly knowing what Stockholm was like in the summer. It's the kind of city that transforms with each season,

and everyone has their favourite time to visit. Besides being the biggest of the Nordic capitals, Stockholm is a city of remarkable diversity. Its architecture ranges from classical buildings to striking examples of modern brutalism. The Stockholm aesthetic spans from traditional romantic styles to sleek industrial minimalism. To truly know Stockholm, you must explore its neighbourhoods and uncover its secrets. Every district has its own unique character, and it takes curiosity to really let the city in. But don’t worry, our Stockholm guide will take you straight to the coolest locations.

KEBAB
& CAFE

Ett Hem
Nobis Hotel Stockholm
Stockholm Stadshotell
Villa Dahlia
Bank Hotel
Berns Hotel
Hobo Hotel
Hotel Skeppsholmen
Hotel At Six

Stay

Ett Hem

Sköldungagatan 2
114 27 Stockholm

@etthemstockholm
ethem.se
+46 820 0590

Home away from home? Ett Hem ("a home" in English) is an intimate boutique hotel nestled in a beautifully restored townhouse in the cozy Östermalm district. Originally built as a private residence in 1910, Ett Hem has undergone a meticulous transformation into a boutique hotel while retaining its original charm. The interiors feature a curated blend of Scandinavian antiques and modern design, crafted by founder Jeanette Mix and designer Ilse Crawford.

The hotel spans three private houses. Sköldungagatan 2 has 12 guest rooms, a cozy living room, a library, and a tranquil garden. Sköldungagatan 4 offers 10 additional rooms and welcoming spaces, while Sköldungagatan 6 provides private residences for long-term stays.

What truly sets Ett Hem apart is its warmth and hospitality, making you feel like a special guest in a private home.

Nobis Hotel Stockholm

Norrmalmstorg 2–4
111 86 Stockholm

@nobishotelstockholm
nobishotel.se
+46 8 614 1000

Nobis hotel is located on Norrmalmstorg, one of Stockholm's most famous squares, occupying two grand 19th-century stone buildings. The hotel's 201 rooms, designed by the renowned Claesson Koivisto Rune, capture the essence of Scandinavian minimalism. Muted tones and warm materials, inspired by Stockholm's winter light, create a calming, home-like atmosphere. Beyond its contemporary style, Nobis has an extraordinary history. In 1973, this was the site of the infamous bank heist that gave birth to the term "Stockholm Syndrome," when hostages developed unexpected sympathy for their captors. Today, this historical site has been transformed into a modern destination where contemporary design and past legacies converge. The hotel's public spaces include a stylishly mismatched lounge with a 28-meter-high ceiling and a 1970s-inspired bar.

Nobis hotel shares the same building as the flagship stores of Acne and Marimekko.

Stockholm Stadshotell

Björngårdsgatan 23
118 52 Stockholm

@stockholmstadshotell
stockholmstadshotell.com
+46 8 165030

What does it take to make a "super" design hotel in Stockholm? Well, first you take the team behind Café Nizza, Johan Agrell, Jon Lacotte, and Dan Källström, then you make them team up with the Swedish-American duo Fredrik Carlström, founder of Alma on Nybrogatan, and Ian Nicholson, known for his work at Mercer Hotel, Chiltern Firehouse, and Chateau Marmont. With such a dream team, expectations can only be sky-high.

In December 2024 Stockholm Stadshotell opened in a historic building dating back to 1875 on Björngårdsgatan in the trendy neighbourhood of Södermalm. With 32 rooms and suites, two restaurants, a bar, a guest lounge, a sauna with a cold plunge, and a courtyard garden restaurant, the hotel is a vibrant destination for both Stockholmers and visitors. Swedish design firm Studio Escapist oversaw the interior design of the guest rooms, lobby, and chambre séparée, ensuring the preservation of the building's historic character and unique charm. The idea was to create something that resembles a family-run hotel, inspired by the traditional Stadshotells in Sweden, offering lodging for travelers and serving as a gathering place for the local community.

The building, dating back to 1873, was commissioned by Queen Dowager Josefina as a place for less fortunate women of noble class.

Villa Dahlia

Tegnérlunden 8
113 59 Stockholm

hotelvilladahlia.com
+46 8 5721 2600

Villa Dahlia, a boutique hotel that opened in 2024, sits gracefully above the leafy Tegnérlunden, right in the heart of Stockholm. It's the third addition to the Malmström/Cappelen family's collection, offering 103 thoughtfully designed rooms and suites, complete with a restaurant, cocktail bar, dedicated spa, fitness studio, and private dining and conference spaces. The Malmström family's hospitality legacy dates back to the 1960s, with their flagship property, Hotel Diplomat, having been crowned "Sweden's Best Hotel" five times by the Condé Nast Traveler Readers' Choice Awards.

Architect Per Öberg has masterfully reimagined the building, transforming it into a space that reflects the elegance of Milanese townhouses from the 1920s and 1930s, during the height of Art Deco. The result is a stunning blend of past and present, where every detail feels both timeless and freshly inspired. Inside, the interior design by mother-daughter duo Anna and Pauline Cappelen features a carefully curated mix of classic and modern objects, sourced from smaller suppliers to ensure quality and uniqueness.

The result is a stunning blend of past and present, where every detail feels both timeless and freshly inspired.

BANK HOTEL

Bank Hotel

Arsenalsgatan 6
111 47 Stockholm

@bankhotelstockholm
bankhotel.se
+46 8 598 58000

Bank Hotel once housed a bank but now invites guests to experience a luxurious stay that blends art-deco flair with Stockholm's modern design sensibility. From the moment you step through its massive bronze doors, the building's history is tangible, yet softened by light-filled spaces and contemporary touches. The former banking hall, now a soaring restaurant with a six-meter glass ceiling, gleams with blue-green stucco and streams of sunlight.

Every detail has been meticulously preserved and reimagined, from Venetian chandeliers to mahogany-clad walls, creating an atmosphere that feels both grand and intimate. Even the dining comes with a twist, like the Bonnie's restaurant, a cheeky nod to Bonnie Parker.

Berns Hotel

Näckströmsgatan 8
111 47 Stockholm

@berns
berns.se
+46 8 566 32000

Since 1863, Berns Hotel has been a key part of Stockholm's cultural landscape, blending its Belle Époque charm with modern style. The historic exterior, once the setting for August Strindberg's Red Room, now welcomes guests into a contemporary space with warm cherry wood and marble accents. The suites offer a touch of extra luxury, some featuring private saunas and interiors by designers like Philippe Starck.

The restaurants and bars, redesigned by Terence Conran, make it one of Stockholm's top performance venues, its concert hall hosts everything from drama to DJs, music acts to stand-up comedy, drawing a different crowd every night. Yet, Berns prides itself on a sense of intimacy. Afterall, 82 rooms make it a modestly sized hotel.

Whether it's the discretion or the buzz, Berns is a celebrity favorite, attracting stars like Lady Gaga, Bob Dylan, Rihanna, Bill Gates, Beyoncé, and the Dalai Lama.

Hobo Hotel

Brunkebergstorg 4
111 51 Stockholm

@hobosthlm
hobo.se
+46 8 5788 2700

In Brunkebergstorg, you'll find not one, but three of Stockholm's coolest hotels, all located right next to each other. Hobo is one of them, a true Gen-Z design hotel built on the concept that traveling should be more than just a place to stay. Opened in 2017, this design hotel redefines what it means to stay in a city, blending modern innovation with a strong sense of community. With 201 rooms tailored for every type of traveler, Hobo is as much a gathering space as it is a hotel. The vibrant interiors, designed by Berlin-based Studio Aisslinger, bring a clean, modern aesthetic with a playful edge. Custom furnishings, like the Hobo sofa created in collaboration with Italian brand Cappellini, add to the cool, laid-back vibe. A standout feature is the hotel's aquaponic system, which grows herbs and produce for its restaurant, merging urban farming with sustainable design. Beyond the rooms, you'll find the popular TAK restaurant and club, the dynamic 5EMMAN event space, and art installations by local designers.

Hobo is more than a hotel. It's a space that connects you with the city, its culture, and its local community.

Hotel Skeppsholmen

Gröna gången 1
111 49 Stockholm

@hotelskeppsholmen
hotelskeppsholmen.se
+46 8 407 2300

Hotel Skeppsholmen is located on the tranquil island of Skeppsholmen. Though just a short walk from the city center, the hotel feels like a peaceful retreat. Built in 1699, this beautifully preserved building is surrounded by lush gardens and offers stunning views of the sea and the city's skyline. Inside, the interiors by Claesson Koivisto Rune feature a clean, minimalist aesthetic that perfectly complements the 17th-century architecture. The hotel has 78 designed rooms, each offering views of either the sea or the gardens. The restaurant at Hotel Skeppsholmen is a favorite among locals, who visit for relaxed meals or to enjoy fika, Sweden's beloved tradition of coffee and cake.

Hotel At Six

Brunkebergstorg 6
111 51 Stockholm

@hotelatsix
hotelatsix.com
+46 8 5788 2800

At Six is perfectly situated in the heart of Stockholm, within the vibrant commercial district of Brunkebergstorg, neighbourhood that, in the 19th century, served as a residential haven for the city's social elite. Set within a striking brutalist building, the hotel offers 343 rooms and suites, from spacious standard rooms to the ultra-exclusive presidential suite. The interiors, crafted by London-based Universal Design Studio, feature a sleek, monochrome palette and museum-worthy art. Upon arrival, guests are greeted by an imposing Jaume Plensa statue, setting the stage for the hotel's artistic ambiance. Throughout the hotel, you will find numerous unique art pieces by Olafur Eliasson, Julian Opie, Sol Le Witt and many more.

They have a great Scandinavian-inspired menu at The Dining Room, while the Blanche & Hierta bar offers one of the city's most extensive wine lists. Head up to the rooftop terrace to enjoy a drink and the panoramic views.

At Six is a five-star experience blending luxury, coolness, art, design and gastronomy.

2

Stora Bageriet
Drop Coffee
Lillebrors Bageri
Restaurant Nationalmuseum
Bambi
Bar Montan
Brutalisten
Bleck
Café Nizza
Persona
Riche Fenix
Gaia Matbar
Solen
Kvarnen
Bar Europa
Kouthoofd Familie Winkel
Svarta Hästen
Tyge & Sessil
Savant Bar
Alba Vinbar

Taste

Stora Bageriet

Sibyllegatan 2
114 51 Stockholm

@stora_bageriet
storabageriet.com
+46 827 7272

Step into history at Stora Bageriet, Stockholm's iconic bakery located in the city's oldest industrial building. Originally known as Kronobageriet, this legendary spot has churned out fresh loaves for over 300 years, once baking up to 60,000 loaves daily to supply the military. Locals affectionately named it Stora Bageriet, a title that now lives on in the newly reopened bakery, located within the Scenkonstmuseet (Performing Arts Museum).

Inside, you'll find an inviting mix of whitewashed walls, wooden tables, and checkered tiles, evoking a timeless charm that pairs beautifully with their buttery rolls and wafer-thin croissants. Each treat is crafted with organic, seasonal ingredients sourced from local producers, making every bite a reflection of Stora Bageriet's dedication to quality.

Since 2023, Stora Bageriet has expanded its reach with a second location in Vasastan, a perfect extension of the original Östermalm charm.

Drop Coffee

Wollmar Yxkullsgatan 10
118 50 Stockholm

@dropcoffeeroasters
dropcoffee.com
+46 7 07779488

Drop Coffee, located near Mariatorget in Stockholm's Södermalm district, is a must-visit for coffee lovers. Founded by Joanna Alm, ranked among the top three roasters in the world, and Stephen Leighton in 2009 as a humble coffee bar, it quickly evolved into an award-winning specialty roastery known for its commitment to quality and sustainability. Today, they roast their own beans in Rosersberg, just north of the city, ensuring each cup tells the story of its origin with a light-to-medium roast that highlights the unique flavors of every bean.

Drop Coffee is the perfect place to start your day with a perfectly brewed coffee and a classic smörgås, an open-faced sandwich. The vibe is relaxed, and the team of knowledgeable baristas is always ready to guide you through the flavors, whether you're a coffee connoisseur or simply looking for a "damn good coffee."

Award-winning coffee experience in the trendy Södermalm district.

DROP COFFEE • ROASTERS
DROP COFFEE

Lillebrors Bageri

Rörstrandsgatan 10
113 40 Stockholm

@lillebrorsbageri
lillebrors.se

Lillebrors Bageri might be tiny, but it's overflowing with charm, warmth, and some of Stockholm's best buns and breads. Since opening in late 2016, this Rörstrandsgatan bakery has been all about creating a positive, inviting space, bringing a small-town warmth to the big city. With a focus on kindness and craftsmanship, Lillebrors aims to make bread that feels like a daily luxury, encouraging guests to connect with the heart of breadmaking.

Inside, a single wooden counter dominates the space, but in the warmer months, patrons can enjoy their coffee and pastries outdoors as the street transforms into a car-free haven. Don't miss their buttery cardamom buns, creamy-filled treats, or the delicious, mouth-melting croissants. Though seating is limited to two outdoor benches, the line snaking along Rörstrandsgatan's historic façades is proof that Lillebrors Bageri's welcoming atmosphere and indulgent bakes are well worth the wait.

Restaurant Nationalmuseum

Södra Blasieholmshamnen 2A
111 48 Stockholm

@nationalmuseumswe
nationalmuseum.se
+46 8480 01810

Restaurant Nationalmuseum is a true fusion of art, design, and Swedish culinary craft, set within Stockholm's National Museum of Fine Arts. Opened after an extensive renovation in 2018, the restaurant occupies three grand galleries that were once closed to the public, with stunning views of Strömmen and the Royal Palace. Here, Swedish chef Fredrik Eriksson combines traditional flavors with modern touches, drawing from ingredients sourced between the 55th and 69th latitudes, all crafted to elevate the dining experience.

The interiors are a design lover's dream. Helmed by designer Matti Klenell and a talented team, the space showcases bespoke furniture, fittings, and tableware that reflect Sweden's rich artistic heritage. The atmosphere is inviting, like a stylish living room where you can settle in for long, social lunches or quick bites in the Glass bar.

This outstanding restaurant even comes with a museum, or is it the other way around?

DOMAINE DE LA
GRANGE DES PERES
2020
ARBOIS
BAMBi BAMBi BAMBi BAMBi
BAMB!
Mazière
CAVALLOTTO
Barolo
Helicon
face b
Marc de Bourgogne
CHARTREUSE

Bambi

Bjurholmsgatan 18
116 83 Stockholm

@bambi_4_ever
bambi.nu
+46 7222 87626

Bambi! Not exactly what you'd expect for a restaurant name, right? But ask the folks behind it, and they'll say it's all about keeping things "fresh", and yes, they serve a fair share of venison too. The vibe is super laid-back and inviting, the kind of place the Swedes affectionately call a "krog," which sits somewhere between a bistro and a tavern.

Bambi made its debut in autumn 2023, down in Södermalm's southern pocket, Skanstull. Word spread fast, as these things do, and soon enough, natural wine aficionados and local foodies were all in on the secret. Expect a tantalising mix of rustic French classics and loud music, all wrapped up in a 1970s-inspired setting with heavy brown furniture and walls splashed in retro green and orange. Bambi is, without a doubt, the distilled essence of Södermalm coolness.

Expect a tantalising mix of rustic French classics and loud music, all wrapped up in a 1970s-inspired setting with heavy brown furniture and walls splashed in retro green and orange.

Bar Montan

Förbindelsehallen
121 62 Johanneshov

@barmontan
barmontan.com
+46 8 84 8000

New York has the Meatpacking District. Copenhagen has Kødbyen. Stockholm has Slakthusområdet, an exciting new urban industrial area in the southern part of the city.

One of its most intriguing new spots is Bar Montan, a small French-inspired bistro. It's a modern kitchen that celebrates traditional, time-tested methods of food preservation and cooking. It's vibrant, fun, and everything tastes superb. If you expect to be guided by the menu, you might be surprised as they often list just the main ingredient. Perhaps it's the kitchen's way of letting the ingredients take center stage.

Bar Montan is another great place in Slakthusområdet. The menu is minimalist, but everything tastes superb.

Brutalisten

Regeringsgatan 71
111 56 Stockholm

@brutalisten
brutalisten.com
+46 7216 18683

Brutalisten isn't your typical Stockholm restaurant. Here, "brutalism" doesn't refer to concrete walls or stark architecture. It's all about the food! Conceived by artist Carsten Höller, Brutalisten brings his long-time vision to life, a culinary experiment rooted in his 2018 *Brutalist Kitchen Manifesto*.

Every dish here is an ode to simplicity and raw flavour, showcasing a philosophy that strips away excess to reveal the true character of each ingredient. Think of it as a lesson in restraint: dishes are crafted with only one ingredient, often accompanied by just water or salt, following a strict "brutalist" approach that honours minimalism. Höller even categorises his creations as *Semi-Brutalist* (a dash of oil and minimal extras), *Brutalist* (nothing but water and salt), and *Ortho-Brutalist* (pure ingredient, no additions). Even the drinks reflect this minimalist ethos. Expect Swedish natural wines, Brutalist-style beers made without hops, and a selection of non-alcoholic options infused with unique flavours, from fruits, flowers, and berries.

Bleck

Katarina Bangata 68
116 42 Stockholm

@restaurang_bleck
restaurangbleck.se

Bleck opened on National Day in 2015 in a space that was once a tool shed for park workers, in a park that few even knew existed. Here, founder Kalle Schröder envisioned a "Swedish bistro" that would breathe new life into this overlooked corner of Ringvägen and Katarina Bangata. Bleck has certainly delivered, quickly becoming one of Södermalm's favourite gathering spots. The menu is minimal but expertly crafted, with just four dishes each night, designed for sharing, plus a popular weekend brunch. Over time, Bleck's outdoor seating has expanded with a spacious terrace, an outdoor bar, and now a glass-enclosed room for year-round dining.

CAFE
7/7 NIZZA
Borgmästargatan
1-7
kv. Signalen
Åsögatan
171-175
kv. Signalen

Café Nizza

Åsögatan 171
116 32 Stockholm

@cafenizza
cafenizza.se
+46 8 640 9950

Any Stockholm guide that wants to be taken seriously would be incomplete without Café Nizza. Since 2016, this iconic Södermalm restaurant has anchored itself in the heart of Stockholm's hipster zone, maintaining a truly original and unpretentious vibe.

Everything here is tastefully low-key. The interior embraces a minimalist Mediterranean bistro aesthetic, a subtle nod to its name, Café Nizza (inspired by Nice on the French Riviera).

The real stars here are the food and the atmosphere. The dishes are created as an amazing blend of Italian and French cuisine. The pasta is exceptional, especially their signature Fermentata Cacio e Pepe. The frequently changing wine list highlights a range of excellent selections from small producers, guaranteeing there's always something fresh to explore.

Persona

Torstenssonsgatan 11
114 56 Stockholm

@personasthlm
personasthlm.com
+46 7357 02731

Persona, inspired by Ingmar Bergman's 1966 film, is a stylish standout in Stockholm's Östermalm, blending high-end dining with a warm, inviting twist. Set within an old townhouse, its historic exterior gives way to an elegant, intimate interior designed by Erik Bratsberg. The space is crafted with natural stone, wood, asymmetrical terrazzo, and touches of patinated brass, creating a vibe that feels more like a refined living room than a traditional restaurant.

The culinary minds behind Persona are French chef Louis Cespedes and sommelier Jonathan Nystrom, who met at Stockholm's celebrated three-Michelin-starred Franzén. Here, Cespedes raises the bar for fine dining with a unique approach: outstanding dishes paired with an atmosphere that's all about ease and welcome. Start your evening by choosing your wine from the cellar, and let the chefs tailor an à la carte experience to match, or opt for the tasting menu to explore the full scope of Persona's world-class flavours.

Persona offers a unique fine dining experience that is truly out of the ordinary.

Riche Fenix

Götgatan 40
118 26 Stockholm

@richefenix
richefenix.se

Riche Fenix is Riche's slightly rowdy little sister, nestled in the heart of Södermalm. Building on Riche's legacy of over 100 years of good food, excellent service, and vibrant cultural ambiance, Riche Fenix brings this experience to a new social spot in Södermalm. Opened in September 2022, it aims to create a lively, fun bar atmosphere with a focus on simple yet high-quality food.

The charm of Riche Fenix lies in its unpretentious approach. While it's straightforward in style, it's marked by carefully curated details and quality that touch every aspect. The food is uncomplicated yet made from the finest ingredients, delivering complex and satisfying flavours. Here, you can enjoy anything from an exclusive glass of wine to a simple draft beer, nothing is too big or too small.

Riche Fenix is inspired by the story of the Phoenix bird, which is reflected throughout the space.

Gaia Matbar

Vattenledningsvägen 44
126 33 Hägersten

@gaia_matbar
gaiamatbar.se
+46 7602 14511

Gaia Matbar brings a laid-back charm to Midsommarkransen, offering a cozy blend of bistro warmth and wine bar allure. With a menu that changes weekly, Gaia keeps things fresh and seasonal, letting you choose between à la carte options or a carefully crafted 4-course set menu, ideal for those who want a little taste of everything.

The wine list is short but sweet. Every bottle is handpicked from small-scale producers who focus on organic and natural practices. And the food? Mostly sourced from organic Swedish farms, with flavour twists from around the globe. Behind it all is a team of ex-hospitality pros, a sommelier and three chefs, bringing their shared passion and expertise to every dish.

Gaia is open Wednesday to Sunday, with lunch served on Fridays and Saturdays. There are always a few drop-in seats at the bar, and in summertime, the large outdoor terrace becomes the perfect spot to linger over dinner or enjoy a glass under the open sky.

Solen

Hallgränd 45
121 62 Stockholm

@solen_sthlm
solen.se
+46 8 1265 3600

Solen, Swedish for "the sun," draws inspiration from warmth, light, and celestial themes, creating a dining experience as radiant as its name suggests. Located in Slakthusområdet, Stockholm's former meatpacking district, Solen brings industrial elegance to life in the historic Hus 26 building. Designed by Stockholm studio Specific Generic, the restaurant's layout mirrors the cosmos, with tables orbiting a central, fire-lit hearth while skylights and clerestory windows flood the space with natural light. Exposed concrete and brass fixtures contrast with soft, rounded benches and greenery, creating cozy zones within the expansive space. A sleek stainless-steel bar and constellation-inspired lighting add a touch of interstellar elegance. Michelin-starred chefs Adam Dahlberg and Albin Wessman lead the culinary vision, crafting a menu inspired by sun-soaked food capitals like Tel Aviv, Naples, and Oaxaca. Embracing fire as a central theme, the menu offers roasted, grilled, and smoked dishes, from Mediterranean-inspired small plates to wood-fired pizzas and tacos.

Located in the Meatpacking District, Solen shines as the new bright star in Stockholm's culinary scene.

Kvarnen

Tjärhovsgatan 4
116 21 Stockholm

@restaurant_kvarnen
kvarnen.com
+46 8643 0380

Kvarnen has been a cornerstone of Södermalm since 1908, a true Stockholm classic with roots as deep as its history. Named after the old "grey mill" *(Gråkvarn)* that once stood nearby, Kvarnen's heritage shines through its warm, no-fuss vibe, staying loyal to Södermalm's working-class spirit. Walking in, you're met with a sense of nostalgia. The grand dining room, with its towering windows, black-and-white checkered floors, and walls filled with quirky details and vintage artwork, feels like a time capsule of old Stockholm. There's even a rustic bar tucked at the back, inviting you to settle in for a well-poured pint or a traditional snaps.

The menu offers the best of traditional and modern Swedish cuisine, with favourites like pickled herring, Swedish meatballs, and toast Skagen, alongside seasonal dishes like reindeer stew, grilled trout, and cured salmon, all crafted with seasonal ingredients.

A favourite with Hammarby football fans in their green-and-white gear, Kvarnen is also known to readers of *The Millennium Trilogy,* where it served as Lisbeth Salander's meeting spot.

Reserved
Ferrari

Bar Europa

Hornsgatan 78
118 21 Stockholm

@bareuropa.eu
bareuropa.eu

Bar Europa began as a casual side project among friends with day jobs but quickly evolved into something much bigger, a communal effort driven by nearly 30 partners united by a simple vision: creating a space where good times and great company are constants in a world that often moves too fast. What might seem like a carefully crafted concept is, in fact, far more organic. True to European tradition, Bar Europa evolves naturally, allowing things to happen without overthinking. Here, spontaneity reigns, and the unplanned often feels effortlessly intentional. While the co-owners may not be seasoned restaurateurs, the kitchen is where their talent shines. The food is simple yet refined, delicious without trying too hard, and always crafted with care. A weekly-changing menu offers an unexpected mix, from snacks to mains and desserts. One thing remains constant, though: a slice of pizza and a crisp lager.

Kouthoofd Familie Winkel

Stora Nygatan 19
111 27 Stockholm

@kouthoofdfamiliewinkel
kouthoofdfamiliewinkel.se

Looking for a cool spot in Gamla Stan? Look no further, Kouthoofd Familie Winkel is the place to be. From the start, this bar has relied on organic growth over traditional marketing, letting word-of-mouth build its reputation as one of Stockholm's best-kept secrets.

Kouthoofd Familie Winkel is the brainchild of Jesper Kouthoofd, a celebrated designer and entrepreneur who co-founded the renowned fashion brand Acne Studios. He has since channeled his creativity into the tech world with Teenage Engineering, a company famous for its groundbreaking electronic music instruments and design.

The bar stands out with its meticulously curated ambiance. A custom-designed sound system and soundproof wooden panels create an unparalleled auditory experience, while the interior blends Italian, German, and Japanese aesthetics.

This great bar with snacks and smaller dishes could just as easily be located on a small street in Tokyo.

Stora Nygatan
kv. Iphigenia
19
kouthoo
familie
winkel

TOTAL CHESS

Svarta Hästen

Biblioteksgatan 21
114 35 Stockholm

@svartahastenschackbar
svartahasten.se

If you're a chess enthusiast with a taste for fine wine, Stockholm has just the spot for you. Svarta Hästen is Sweden's first wine bar dedicated to chess. It's nestled in the historic basement of Arnoldshuset, combining the art of the game with the elegance and joy of wine.

The atmosphere is both relaxed and refined. Grab a glass, settle in, and challenge yourself on custom chess boards crafted by Gothenburg artist Kim Björnson. With space for 20 devoted players and plenty of room for casual visitors, Svarta Hästen is as inviting as it is unique. Sommelier Calle Stuborn, a former junior chess champion, has curated a wine list that pairs classic French sophistication with the vibrant allure of natural wines.

Enjoy a late-night chess match with a good glass of wine at Svarta Hästen, perfectly nestled in the heart of Stureplan.

Beach
Master
Horny
FRUKT-
STEREO

Tyge & Sessil

Brahegatan 4
114 37 Stockholm

@tygesessil
tygesessil.se
+46 8 519 42277

Tyge & Sessil, located near Stureplan in central Stockholm, is a busy wine café with a casual atmosphere that stands out in this otherwise upscale neighbourhood. Opened in 2016 by renowned chef Niklas Ekstedt, the café champions the underdogs of the wine world, showcasing natural wines from independent, small-scale producers. The wine list highlights lesser-known grapes and regions, inviting guests to explore beyond the traditional.

Co-founded with sommelier Maximilian Mellfors, Tyge & Sessil was born from a desire for an accessible, slightly chaotic venue with a wide selection of exciting wines. Guided by the concept of glouglou, an unpretentious, joyful way of enjoying light, low-alcohol natural wines, the café embraces a welcoming and dynamic vibe.

Instead of a traditional bar, a central bench fosters interaction between sommeliers and guests.

Tyge & Sessil is one of the best places to go in Stockholm for wines from small-scale and independent producers.

savant bar

Savant Bar

Tegnérgatan 4
113 58 Stockholm

@savantbar
savantbar.se
+46 7 6021 2630

Savant Bar is one of Stockholm's most iconic natural wine bars offering a unique blend of natural wines, seasonal food, and a passion for music. The bar is renowned for its dynamic wine selection, featuring a daily rotation of wines by the glass and an extensive bottle list with over 500 options, available on their website for wine enthusiasts to explore.

The menu here is all about seasonality and sustainability, with dishes built around organic, locally sourced vegetables, primarily from Swedish farms. Designed to be shared or enjoyed solo, the food complements the wine perfectly, creating a culinary experience that feels both thoughtful and relaxed. Savant Bar operates on a no-reservations basis, with one exception: an exclusive chef's table for those looking to elevate their evening.

Savant bar is a perfect combination of seasonal food,
great music and the appreciation of natural wines.

savant bar
savant bar
Wi FI
SAVANT BAR
DAGENS LUNCH
SNACKS
CORNICHONS 35
MARCONA MANDLAR 50
GRÖNA OLIVER 50
SARDELLER 75
SURDEGSBRÖD 75
DAGENS
-FATOUCH 100
125
125
-SERVERAS MED HEMBAKAT SURDEGSBRÖD
LUNCHVIN 75:-

ALBA
ONNIE) C05T45 G1FT 5H0P

Alba Vinbar

Skånegatan 88
116 37 Stockholm

@alba_nytorget
albavinbar.se
+46 836 9650

Tucked away in Södermalm's vibrant streets, Alba Vinbar feels like Stockholm's best-kept secret. Most of the crowd are locals and wine lovers who've stumbled upon this cosy spot. It's pretty tiny, but the wine bar has a perfectly homely vibe, that can't be designed or bought. Weekend evenings at Alba feel more like someone's hosting a private party, as the waiters keep squeezing in extra chairs and tables as needed.

Opened in 2021, Alba quickly became a neighbourhood favourite, and it's easy to see why. The wine list is thoughtfully curated, featuring natural wines from small European producers, all at reasonable prices. The food menu consists of a relaxed, rustic mix of French and Italian bites that pairs perfectly with the wine selection.

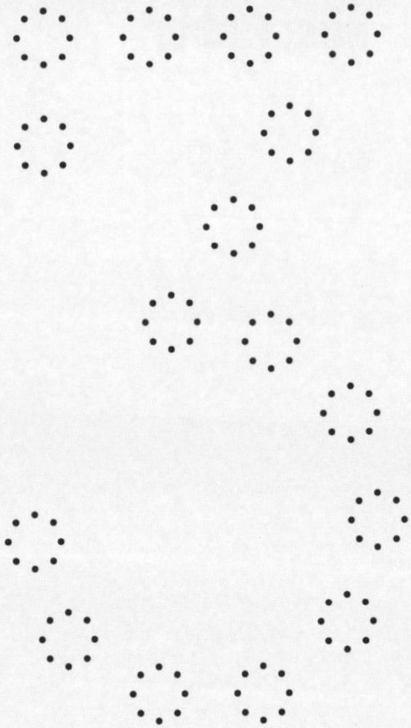

A Days March
Konst-ig
All Blues
Acne Studios
Ettresex / Jade
Dusty Deco
Grandpa
Sneakersnstuff
Stora Skuggan
Tambur
Flattered
Svenskt Tenn
Östermalms Saluhall

Shop

A Days March

Åsögatan 126
116 24 Stockholm

@adaysmarch
adaysmarch.se
+46 7 0274 6572

A Day's March, founded in 2014 by Marcus Gårdö, Pelle Lundquist, and Stefan Pagréus, is a Swedish clothing label that combines function with style. The name itself is a nod to an old military term, referring to the distance an army can cover in a single day, symbolizing their goal to create clothing that carries you through the triumphs and challenges of everyday life.

Their flagship store is housed in a striking 1930s functionalist building on Åsögatan, in the heart of Södermalm. Inside, the design is a seamless blend of modern minimalism and vintage charm. The interior mirrors the building's "funkis" style with clean, straight lines, while large windows framed by concrete pillars invite natural light. Adding a touch of artistry, a round-shaped cashier desk and steel-framed glass block walls with circular patterns echo the modernist aesthetic of Paris's iconic Maison de Verre.

konst-ig
OBS

Konst-ig

Åsögatan 124
116 24 Stockholm

@konstig_bokhandel
konstigbooks.com
+46 8 204520

Konst-ig, located on Åsögatan in the heart of Södermalm, is one of Scandinavia's leading art bookstores, serving as a vital hub for Stockholm's creative community since its founding in 1994. Specializing in a wide range of visual art forms, from architecture and graphic design to photography and fashion, the store offers an impressive selection of books, magazines, and journals on topics as diverse as European street art, cubism, brutalism, classic fonts, and even album cover design.

More than just a bookstore, Konst-ig is a cultural destination. It regularly hosts book launches and talks, attracting artists, designers, and enthusiasts alike. The shop also provides consultancy services, offering expert advice to institutions and individuals on building specialized art libraries.

Konst-ig's curated selection of books makes it an essential stop for anyone passionate about design, art and architecture.

konst-ig

All Blues™

All Blues

Birger Jarlsgatan 2
114 34 Stockholm

@allbluesofficial
allblues.se
+46 8 402 0921

All Blues, a jewellery brand founded in Stockholm in 2010 by Fredrik Nathorst and Jacob Skragge, has built a name for its minimalist, handcrafted designs. Every piece is handcrafted by a family-run goldsmith atelier, now in its third generation, using locally sourced, recycled precious metals. With a focus on ethical production and sustainability, each piece reflects the founders' vision of understated luxury.

In 2020, All Blues took things to the next level with the opening of their flagship store on Birger Jarlsgatan in Östermalm, one of Stockholm's chicest neighbourhoods. Housed in a 19th-century building, the space has been reimagined with a minimalist edge, thanks to architect Jack Dalla Santa. What used to be a two-storey layout has been transformed into one expansive, airy room. At the centre, a glass house delicately displays the jewellery collection, juxtaposed against sleek mirrors, steel accents, and the smooth white terrazzo floor, creating an atmosphere that's as bold as it is serene.

Jewellery brand All Blues' flagship store combines glass, mirrors, and steel to create a bold, minimalist experience.

Acne Studios
2
tudios
Ac

Acne Studios

Norrmalmstorg 2
111 46 Stockholm

@acnestudios
acnestudios.com
+46 8 558 50510

If Swedish fashion is your thing, a visit to Stockholm wouldn't be complete without stopping by Acne Studios' flagship store on Norrmalmstorg Square or, for that matter, the cult-favorite Acne Archive in Vasastan.

Acne Studios emerged in 1996, born from the creative collective ACNE, which dabbled in everything from graphic design to film and advertising. It all began in 1997 when co-founder Jonny Johansson crafted 100 pairs of raw denim jeans with a signature red stitch, gifting them to friends and family. Soon, magazines like *Wallpaper** and *Vogue Paris* took notice, and the brand skyrocketed into the fashion spotlight. The flagship store sits on historic ground at Norrmalmstorg Square, in the very building that once housed Sveriges Kreditbanken. Yes, the same building infamous for the hostage situation that coined the term "Stockholm Syndrome." Acne Studios' signature minimalist style blends perfectly with echoes of history, creating a unique shopping experience.

AALTO
SUN RA
Tillmans
Reader
WaxPoetics
PATCH & TWEAK

Ettresex / Jade

Åsögatan 136
116 24 Stockholm

@ettresex
ettresex.com

@jaderecordings
jaderecordings.com

Tucked away at Åsögatan 136, you'll find not one but two hotspots in Stockholm's fashion and music scene: Ettresex and Jade. Ettresex, established in 2017 by Emilian Minas and Marcus Winter, has quickly become a go-to for those who appreciate a well-curated selection of pre-owned designer and vintage fashion. Specialising in pieces from the '80s to early 2000s, this boutique is a treasure trove of designer brands and unique vintage apparel from Europe, the US, and Japan, a perfect spot for anyone looking to hunt down rare Prada, Rei Kawakubo, or Junya Watanabe pieces.

Right next door is Jade, a fresh addition to the neighbourhood, opening its doors in 2024. This record shop complements Ettresex perfectly with its equally sharp, minimalist aesthetic. Here, you'll discover a well-curated selection of vinyl, with Hip Hop, House, and R&B setting the tone, alongside a few handpicked books and zines to complete the vibe.

Ettresex and Jade have become must-visit spots for Stockholm's fashion crowd, blending style and culture under one roof.

Neighbourhoods

Södermalm
Vasastan
Östermalm
Gamla Stan
Slakthusområdet
Norrmalm
Djurgården
Skeppsholmen

Stockholm

HOUSE of BURGERS
CRONAN
SALLYS

A cityscape is defined by the sum of its neighbourhoods. They are the heartbeat of a city, infusing life and diversity into its very soul. Some are artsy and vibrant, others are more serene and exclusive. Each neighbourhood has its own unique character, and we all have our favourite areas that we feel connected to. In this section, we break down the city and introduce you to the coolest neighbourhoods. All the locations in the book, along with a few bonus spots, are marked on detailed neighbourhood maps, making it easy for you to discover your favourite district.

5
16
15
4
7
11
3
17
2
14
10
13
12
9
8
1
6

Södermalm

1 Bambi (p. 63)
2 Kvarnen (p. 91)
3 Café Nizza (p. 75)
4 Drop Coffee (p. 53)
6 Bar Europa (p. 93)
7 Bleck (p. 73)
8 Riche Fenix (p. 81)
9 Alba Vinbar (p. 111)
10 Grandpa (p. 135)
10 A Days March (p. 115)
11 Tambur (p. 145)
12 Konst-ig (p. 117)
13 Sneakersnstuff (p. 137)
14 Ettresex / Jade (p. 127)
15 Stora Skuggan (p. 141)
16 Fotografiska Museum (p. 173)
17 Stockholm Stadshotell (p. 25)

Södermalm, the large island just south of Gamla Stan, has undergone a remarkable transformation. Once a working-class district, it has evolved into a lively hub now beloved by Stockholm's younger creative crowd. Folkungagatan splits the neighbourhood in two, with the trendy SoFo lying "south of Folkungagatan" and the almost as trendy NoFo conveniently located "North of Folkungagatan". Known simply as "Söder" by the locals, the area has become a haven for designer boutiques, art galleries, coffee shops, bars, and restaurants. You could easily spend the entire weekend exploring all the great spots, both well-known and hidden. Even with this guide in your hand, you will most likely have to cope with a feeling of FOMO, as you only managed to visit half the destinations on your list.

5
4
9
7
8
3
10
2
6
1
11

Vasastan

1 Villa Dahlia (p. 29)
2 Lillebrors Bageri (p. 57)
3 Savant Bar (p. 107)
4 Norra Tornen (p. 183)
5 Carl Eldhs Ateljémuseum (p. 165)
6 Sven-Harrys Konstmuseum (p. 187)

Don't miss:

7 Acne Archive, Torsgatan 53, 113 37
8 Tennstopet, Dalgatan 50, 113 24
9 Systraarna Andersson, Karlbergsvägen 45, 113 37
10 Banacado, Tegnérgatan 6, 113 58
11 Tegnérlunden, Tegnérlunden 8, 113 59

If you're looking to experience everyday life in Stockholm, Vasastan is the place. An upscale neighbourhood with beautiful early 20th-century architecture, fairly priced coffee shops and plenty of green spaces. Vasastan has a cosy, residential feel, but there are also cultural spots to discover. Highlights include Sven-Harry's Art Museum and Carl Eldh's Ateljémuseum, both featured in this guide. Vasastan also has a more lively side. It's a popular spot for grabbing a drink after work or dining at one of the many restaurants. You'll also find small boutiques and vintage shops scattered throughout the area. A retail hotspot is the Acne Archive store on Torsgatan, where you can find great bargains. The district is also well-known for its parks, particularly Vasaparken and Tegnérlunden, which are favourite spots for enjoying outdoor lunches in the summer.

STOCKHOLMS STADSBIBLIOTEK
ARKITEKT GUNNAR ASPLUND 1928

1
14
12
9
11
13
5
6
8
10
4
3
7
2

Östermalm

Don't Miss:

11 Saturnus, Eriksbergsgatan 6, 114 30

12 Tössebageriet, Karlavägen 77, 114 49

13 Broms, Karlavägen 76, Grevgatan 64, 114 59

14 Trattoria Montanari, Grev Turegatan 56, 114 38

Östermalm is one of Stockholm's most upscale neighbourhoods, drawing both locals and visitors. Once known as Ladugårdslandet, or "the barn land," the area underwent a transformation in the 19th century when a new urban plan gave it both its current name and a touch of sophistication. The growing bourgeoisie flocked to the district, constructing grand residences along the waterfront. By the 1930s, sleek modernist buildings with their clean, square lines began to emerge, shaping not just Östermalm but urban design worldwide.

The iconic Östermalms Saluhall is not just a 19th-century architectural landmark; it's also a must-visit destination for food enthusiasts. This vibrant market overflows with culinary delights, complemented by an array of exceptional restaurants and artisan bakeries. While officially part of the neighbouring Norrmalm area, the Bibliotekstan shopping district straddles the border between the two, its upscale boutiques and international luxury brands extending into Östermalm.

ALL
MENY

4
3
2
1

Gamla Stan

			Don't Miss:
1	Kouthoofd Familie Winkel (p. 95)	2	Pharmarium, Stortorget 7, 111 29
		3	Stortorget, Stortorget, 111 29
		4	The Royal Palace, Kungliga slottet, 107 70

Gamla Stan is a small island nestled between the "mainland" and Södermalm. As the name suggests, it's Stockholm's old town, originally founded back in the 13th century. This makes Gamla Stan one of the largest preserved medieval towns in Europe. While many of the original buildings have been replaced with newer ones from the 17th and 18th centuries, the charm remains. In many ways, it feels like a living museum, and that's exactly how Gamla Stan should be experienced. If you're drawn to the old-world atmosphere and cultural treasures, including the Royal Palace, it's worth a visit. More than anything, though, Gamla Stan is a cosy spot, with a few excellent wine and cocktail bars that you'll find featured in this guide.

THE
BISHOPS ARMS

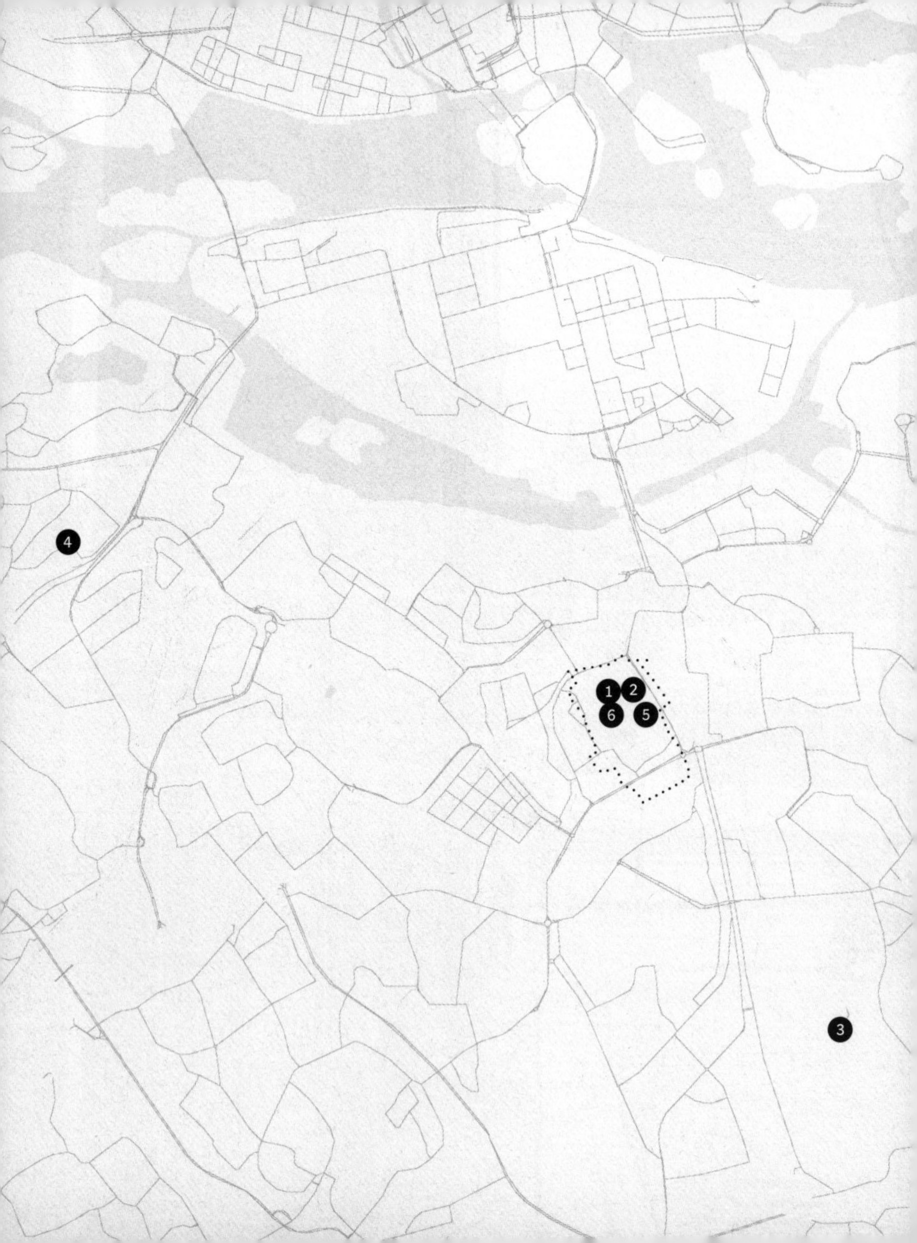
4
1
2
6
5
3

Slakthusområdet

Don't miss:

1 Solen (p. 87)
2 Bar Montan (p. 67)
3 Skogskyrkogården (p. 185)
4 Gaia Matbar (p. 85)
5 Hosoi, Förbindelsehallen, 121 62 Johanneshov
6 Stockholm Roast, Hallvägen 9, 121 62 Johanneshov

Slakthusområdet, once Stockholm's bustling meatpacking district, is rapidly transforming into the city's new hotspot for food, drinks, and music. Located just 10 minutes south of the city center by metro, the area is following in the footsteps of cities like New York and Copenhagen, where former industrial zones have been repurposed into vibrant cultural hubs. What sets Slakthusområdet apart is its thoughtful approach to development: rather than beginning with apartment buildings, the focus has been on creating a lively environment with restaurants, bars, and entertainment venues first, shaping a fresh narrative for the district. The area is home to exciting new spots like Solen and Bar Montan, both featured in this guide. You could easily spend a full day here, especially if you add another growing hotspot, Midsommarkransen, to your itinerary. A standout in Midsommarkransen is Gaia Matbar, a fresh new restaurant making waves with its innovative approach to food and wine.

SLA

USOMRÅDET
Nya Slakthusområde
40

11
6
9
10
8
2
7
13
12
3
1
4
5

Norrmalm

			Don't Miss:
1	Hotel at Six (p. 45)	9	Toteme, Biblioteksgatan 5, 111 46
2	Nobis Hotel Stockholm (p. 21)	10	Byredo, Mäster Samuelsgatan 6, 111 44
3	Berns Hotel (p. 33)	11	Centralbadet, Drottninggatan 88, 111 36
4	Hobo Hotel (p. 39)	12	Arket, Drottninggatan 53, 111 21
5	Nationalmuseum (p. 59)	13	H&M, Drottninggatan 56, 111 21
6	Brutalisten (p. 71)		
7	Acne Studios (p. 125)		
8	Flattered (p. 149)		

Norrmalm is Stockholm's business district and commercial center, filled with high-street fashion along Drottninggatan. A stop at the Arket and H&M flagship stores is considered a must if you're into Swedish fashion.

However, it's not the most beautiful part of the city, as it's dominated by modern buildings constructed between 1950 and 1970. But there are exceptions. Brunkebergstorg is a secluded and calm square, just a few hundred meters away from the bustling shopping streets. The square offers a mix of architectural styles, from neoclassical buildings of the late 1800s to fortress-like brutalist structures from the 1960s. Hotel At Six is located in a former bank with a striking brutalist façade, while the HOBO hotel is housed in a cool, converted 1970s building. Both locations are featured in this guide.

2
4
1
5

Djurgården

			Don't Miss:
1	Liljevalchs (p. 175)	3	Rosendals Trädgårdskafé, Rosendalsterrassen 12, 115 21
2	Museum of Spirits (p. 179)	4	Spritmuseum Restaurant, Djurgårdsstrand 9, 115 21
		5	ABBA The Museum, Djurgårdsvägen 68, 115 21

I don't want to either oversell or undersell Djurgården. In my experience, you visit with a clear purpose in mind, though that could be anything: cultural exploration, a peaceful retreat, or pure entertainment. If following the beaten path Djurgården is undoubtedly Stockholm's most popular tourist destination, filled with must-see spots, the Vasa Museum, Nordiska Museet, and, for those inclined, the world-famous ABBA Museum and Gröna Lund amusement park. But Djurgården also offers more refined cultural experiences such as Liljevalchs Museum and the Museum of Spirits, which are featured in this guide. While it didn't make the list, Rosendals Trädgårdskafé is also highly recommended for a delicious Swedish lunch.

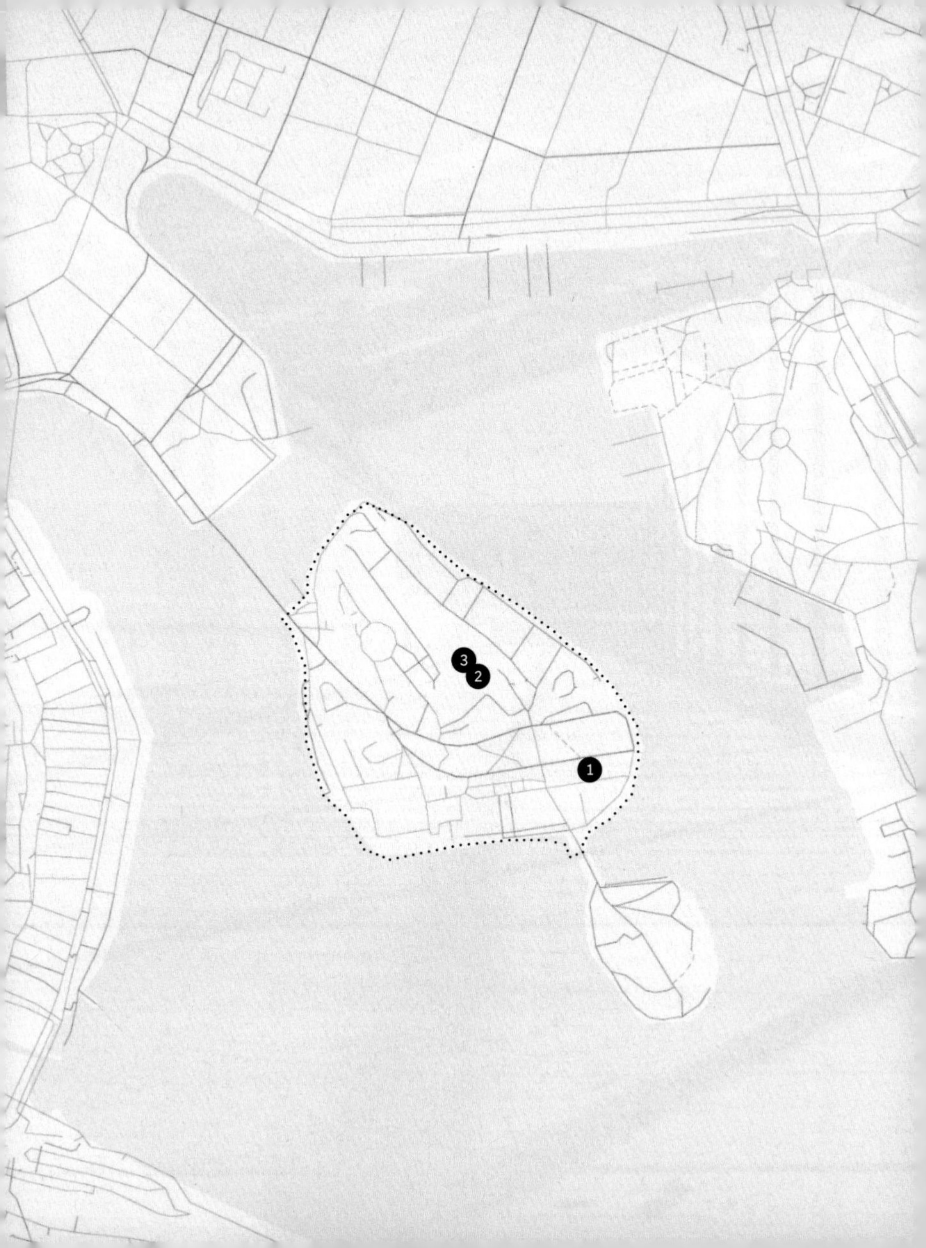
3
2
1

Skeppsholmen

Don't Miss:

1 Hotel Skeppsholmen (p. 43)

2 ArkDes (p. 169)

3 Moderna Museet, Exercisplan 4, 111 49

Skeppsholmen is a hidden gem in central Stockholm, offering a serene escape just minutes from the city's busy streets. While often overshadowed by its more famous neighbour, Djurgården, Skeppsholmen has plenty to offer.

The island is home to ArkDes, Sweden's national center for architecture and design, and Moderna Museet, Stockholm's renowned museum of modern art. Both are must-sees for architecture and art enthusiasts. If you're looking for a stylish stay, Hotel Skeppsholmen, a charming design hotel nestled in historic 17th-century buildings, is a perfect choice for a quite sleep in cozy surroundings. So, before the rumour of this secret spot hits the mainstream, make your way to Skeppsholmen to explore cutting-edge design and art.

Dusty Deco

Linnégatan 13
114 47 Stockholm

@dustydeco
dustydeco.com

Dusty Deco is a prominent Swedish brand and a true paradise for collectors and vintage lovers. The shop features Dusty Deco's own collections of furniture, rugs, and décor, alongside select vintage pieces and curated artworks from Loyal Gallery and Public Service Gallery. Located in the heart of the Östermalm neighbourhood, near high-end designer labels, a few quick turns will lead you straight to Dusty Deco. Founders Edin and Lina Kjellvertz began Dusty Deco as a hobby, with their basements and storage rooms filled to the brim. It soon evolved into a weekend pop-up shop in Gärdet, and now, three years later, they have two fantastic locations, one in Stockholm and a showroom in Palma, Spain.

Dusty Deco is a stylish design store where vintage furniture meets contemporary art.

KINFOLK
NATURAL SOAP
NATURAL SOAP
TINT
TINT

Grandpa

Södermannagatan 21
116 40 Stockholm

grandpastore.se
+46 10 516 44 80

Grandpa started as a vision among friends, more than just a shop, they dreamed of creating a space that felt like a community.

They wanted a spot where people could come together, feel inspired, and enjoy a personal, welcoming atmosphere. And in 2003, they brought that dream to life, opening their first store in Stockholm's Södermalm. It quickly became a neighborhood favorite, known for its unique vibe and friendly service.

Two decades on, Grandpa is still going strong, a local fixture offering a carefully curated selection of fashion and lifestyle products with a focus on timeless design and sustainable values. Recently, their vintage collection has made a much-celebrated return, with hidden gems now waiting to be discovered in the basement of the Södermalm store.

Today, Grandpa is a cornerstone of the local scene, with stores in Gothenburg and Malmö as well.

Sneakersnstuff

Åsögatan 124
116 24 Stockholm

@sneakersnstuff
sneakersnstuff.com

Founded in 1999 by Erik Fagerlind and Peter Jansson out of a love and curiosity for the culture and lifestyle surrounding sneakers, art, music, and sports, Sneakersnstuff has become one of the world's leading sneaker retailers, offering a curated selection of sought-after releases, limited editions, and collaborations.

Located on Åsögatan in the heart of Södermalm, Sneakersnstuff's Stockholm store was the first of four to open in Europe and has established itself as the go-to destination in Stockholm for the latest sneaker and streetwear releases. The store offers a wide range of popular styles from brands such as Adidas Originals, Nike, Jordan Brand, New Balance, PUMA, and more.

If you're seeking the latest releases in sneakers and streetwear, Sneakersnstuff is the place to be.

Stora Skuggan

Östgötagatan 18
116 25 Stockholm

@storaskuggan
storaskuggan.com

Stora Skuggan is a Stockholm-based perfume studio that began as a project among five multidisciplinary creatives. Since launching in 2015, they have established themselves as a niche fragrance house that reimagines the art of perfume-making. Presented in sleek glass bottles with oversized orb caps, each fragrance's packaging is distinguished by unique visuals that unfold through three dimensions: a conceptual idea, a wearable artwork, and an aesthetic object, together reflecting the diverse backgrounds of the collective's members.

Drawing inspiration from history, mysticism, pop culture, and beyond, Stora Skuggan merges curious fascinations with playful wit to create truly distinct olfactory experiences.

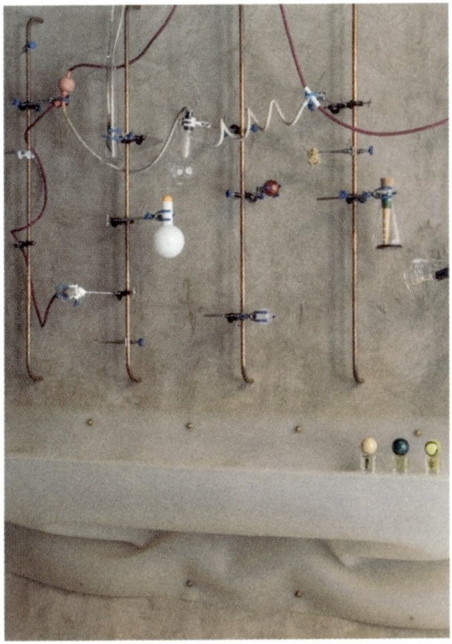

Handcrafted in Stockholm, each Stora Skuggan fragrance is like a small, enchanting masterpiece.

Tambur

Folkungagatan 85
116 22 Stockholm

@tamburstore
tamburstore.se
+46 8 742 8100

Located in the Södermalm district, Tambur offers a thoughtfully curated shopping experience. Founded by designer Anders Widegren and stylist Sebastian Bergström, this small and cozy concept store is designed to feel like a home, with distinct sections resembling a kitchen, dining area, and living room. Tambur focuses on Scandinavian design while also incorporating a selection of globally sourced items, such as handcrafted glassware from Czechoslovakia and brass accessories from Japan.

The store specializes in a range of high-quality home goods, including both decorative objects and practical kitchenware. Sustainability is central to Tambur's approach, with all products carefully selected for their eco-friendly production and free from harmful chemicals. The selection emphasizes local craftsmanship, offering timeless, functional pieces that balance beauty and practicality.

Tambur's commitment to sustainability and quality makes it a go-to destination for those seeking unique items to enhance their home.

Flattered

Mäster Samuelsgatan 11
111 44 Stockholm

@flattered
flattered.com
0046 8 1214 7167

Opened in 2024, the Swedish shoe brand Flattered now resides among other high-end labels in the fashionable Bibliotekstan district. Flattered was founded in 2013 by Stockholm-based entrepreneurs Gustav Lidén and Hanna Kwiatowska Tisner, originally crafting ballerina flats. Since then, the brand has continuously expanded both in size and product range, evolving into an established high-end fashion label that designs handmade shoes and accessories.

The store's interior was designed by Studio Escapist, a local architectural firm that also created the interior for the new Stockholm Stadshotell (p.47). The Flattered retail space features handmade Italian terracotta floors, black accents, linseed oil-treated metalwork, raw-cut curtains, and warm maple furniture. A carefully curated combination of materials and textures reflects a warm yet modern Scandinavian aesthetic.

A carefully curated combination of materials and textures reflects a warm yet modern Scandinavian aesthetic.

Svenskt Tenn

Strandvägen 5
114 51 Stockholm

@svenskttenn
svenskttenn.com
+46 8 670 1600

Svenskt Tenn's flagship store on Strandvägen is an essential destination for design enthusiasts visiting Stockholm. Founded in 1924 by the visionary Estrid Ericson, this iconic Swedish brand has become a cornerstone of Scandinavian interior design. When Austrian architect and designer Josef Frank joined in 1934, he introduced his expertise in vibrant patterns and timeless furniture, contributing significantly to the company's enduring legacy.

Entering the store feels like entering a living gallery of modern classics, bold, colorful prints line the walls, while meticulously crafted furniture invites you to explore. From hand-blown glass and ceramics to contemporary pieces by emerging designers, there's always something new to discover.

SALUHALL

Östermalms Saluhall

Östermalshallen 31
114 39 Stockholm

@ostermalmshallen
ostermalmshallen.se

Like most European capitals, Stockholm can also pride itself on a magnificent food hall. Östermalm's Saluhall's cultural and historical heritage is evident in its architecture and preserved within its walls, making the building exceptionally special. However, its age had created a significant need for refurbishment. After an extensive renovation, Östermalm's Saluhall re-opened in 2020. The old brick building from 1888 now stands more beautiful than ever, serving as one of the most remarkable food venues in Europe. Here, you can experience a taste of Sweden in a historic setting. With butchers, cheesemongers, and small patisserie spots, this is a paradise for foodies.

With butchers, cheesemongers, and small patisserie spots, this is a paradise for foodies.

BÄTTRE TUNNT ÖL ÄN TOMMA KAR
3
2
BEIRUT CAFÉ
BEIRUT CAFÉ
BEIRUT CAFÉ

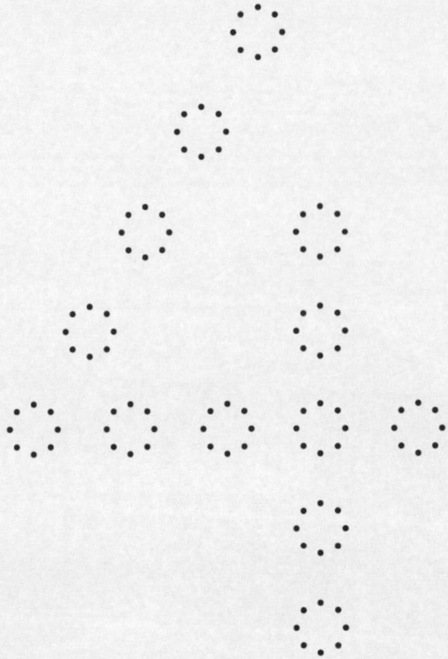

Artipelag
Carl Eldhs Ateljémuseum
ArkDes
Fotografiska
Liljevalchs
Museum of Spirits
Norra Tornen
Skogskyrkogården
Sven-Harrys Konstmuseum
Tensta Konsthall

Explore

Artipelag

Artipelagstigen 1
134 40 Gustavsberg

@artipelag
artipelag.se
+46 8 570 130 00

A 30-minute drive from Stockholm may seem like a trek, but Artipelag makes it more than worth the journey. Located in the scenic archipelago on Värmdö, Artipelag is a unique venue for art, architecture, design, events and top-quality food in a beautiful archipelago landscape. Since its opening in 2012, Artipelag has gained international recognition for its thought-provoking exhibitions and captivating surroundings. Designed by the late architect Johan Nyrén, the museum's building harmonizes beautifully with the landscape, spanning 10,000 square meters and surrounded by 22 acres of pristine forest and waterfront. The interior gallery space of 3,000 square meters has showcased works by renowned artists like William Wegman and Candida Höfer.

The name "Artipelag" cleverly combines "Art," and "Archipelago," reflecting its mission to create a space where art, culture, and nature are joined one holistic experience.

Artipelag is a contemporary arts center set on an island in the Stockholm archipelago.

Carl Eldhs Ateljémuseum

Lögebodavägen 10
113 47 Stockholm

@carleldhsateljemuseum
eldhsatelje.se
+46 8 612 6560

Carl Eldhs Ateljémuseum offers an intimate glimpse into the life and artistry of Carl Eldh (1873–1954), one of Sweden's leading sculptors of the early 20th century.

Set within Eldh's former studio, the museum is a treasure trove of nearly 500 works, ranging from delicate plaster sketches to striking sculptures in bronze, stone, and clay. At the heart of the collection is Eldh's passion for portraiture, with notable depictions of figures like August Strindberg, complemented by his tools, personal memorabilia, and a private art collection featuring works from fellow artists and friends.

The museum's unique atmosphere owes much to Eldh's daughter, Brita, who transformed the studio into a museum after his death. For over 45 years, she carefully preserved its charm, hosting cultural gatherings among the artworks. Today, the museum continues to honour her vision, offering a space where art, history, and community seamlessly come together.

Set within Carl Eldh's former studio, the museum
is a treasure trove of nearly 500 works.

ArkDes

Exercistplan 4
11 49 Stockholm

@arkdesc
arkdes.se
+46 8 5202 3500

ArkDes is a go-to spot for anyone interested in architecture and design. Its full name, The Swedish Centre for Architecture and Design, might be a bit of a mouthful, but this place truly lives up to its reputation. Located on the idyllic island of Skeppsholmen, ArkDes is surrounded by some of Stockholm's most iconic cultural landmarks, yet it stands out for its unique blend of art, architecture, and forward-thinking design.

Past exhibitions have featured legends like Josef Frank and even fashion icon Jean Paul Gaultier, showcasing the gallery's ability to merge different styles and eras. Whether you're an architecture enthusiast or just curious about contemporary design, ArkDes delivers plenty of inspiration. And the next best part? It's free.

ArkDes, located on the island Skeppsholmen, is the Swedish national museum for architecture and design.

Ark
Des

Fotografiska
BUSS

Fotografiska

Stadsgårdshamnen 22
116 45 Stockholm

@fotografiska.stockholm
fotografiska.com
+46 8 5090 0500

Fotografiska is a unique destination for photography, housed in a stunning Art Nouveau building perched along the Södermalm waterfront. Fotografiska has been at the heart of contemporary photography since 2010. Inside, this internationally renowned space hosts an impressive lineup of exhibitions, around 25 each year, featuring iconic names like Annie Leibovitz, Sebastião Salgado, and Ren Hang, alongside emerging talents.

Fotografiska's reach extends far beyond Stockholm, with sister museums now in New York, Tallinn, Shanghai, and Berlin, curating hundreds of thought-provoking exhibitions worldwide. Its mission is clear: to inspire a more conscious world through the power of photography. And let's not forget the top-floor café, offering one of Stockholm's best panoramic views, perfect for a coffee break overlooking the city skyline.

Liljevalchs

Djurgårdsvägen 60
Falkenbergsgatan 3
115 21 Stockholm

@liljevalchs
liljevalchs.se
+46 8 5083 1330

Liljevalchs has been a cornerstone of Stockholm's art scene since 1916, when it first opened its doors as Sweden's very first public gallery dedicated to contemporary art. Nestled on the picturesque island of Djurgården, the gallery continues to live up to its original mission, to showcase the most inspiring and relevant contemporary art. Designed by architect Carl Bergsten, the historic building is an architectural landmark, blending into the scenic surroundings.

Fast forward to 2021, and Liljevalchs entered a bold new chapter with the addition of Liljevalchs+. This striking extension, brought to life by renowned architect Gert Wingårdh and glass designer Ingegerd Råman, adds a fresh, modern edge to the gallery. With its sharp lines and innovative design, Liljevalchs+ perfectly complements the original building while offering a space that pushes boundaries, much like the art it hosts.

For more than a Century, Liljevalchs Konsthall has been the leading exhibition venue for contemporary art in Stockholm.

BITTER ORANGE SNAPS
BÄSK
ARRACK PUNSCH

Museum of Spirits

Djurgårdsvägen 9
115 21 Stockholm

@spritmuseum
spritmuseum.se
+46 8 1213 1300

Spritmuseum is where Swedish drinking culture and history collide in the most engaging, and let's be honest, very Swedish way. I mean, where else but Sweden would you build a museum dedicated to spirits? Established in 1967, this interactive spot in Stockholm is perfect for anyone curious about the nation's spirited past, quite literally.

The star attraction is Sweden: Spirits of a Nation, a permanent exhibition that lets you dive into the world of distilling, explore the heady scents of spices and spirits, and uncover how Sweden's historic drinking habits have shaped modern culture. Spritmuseum also hosts two rotating exhibitions each year to keep things fresh. One highlight is the Absolut Art Collection, showcasing the legendary ad campaign that made Absolut Vodka a global icon, and gave Andy Warhol a run for his money.

With more than 13,000 objects, Spritmuseum offers a fun and boozy journey through Sweden's drinking traditions.

ABSOLUT
VODKA
ABSOLUT WARHOL.
H H
H-C-C-O-H
H H
SMÖRJER DU
KUGGARNA MED
ALKOHOL

Norra Tornen

Torsplan 8
113 65 Stockholm

@oma.eu
oma.com
+31 10 243 82 00

Stockholm's northern skyline has undergone a dramatic transformation, crowned by the striking silhouette of Norra Tornen. For years now, these two awe-inspiring high-rises have captured the attention of the global architectural community, earning nominations in prestigious competitions like the International Highrise Award 2020. Norra Tornen, or the Northern Towers, stand as the tallest residential buildings in Stockholm's city centre. Comprised of two towers, Helix and Innovationen, they were brought to life by the renowned architectural firm OMA, commissioned by Oscar Properties. Completed in 2020, these towers represent a bold blend of functionality, innovation, and artistry. Designed by Reinier de Graaf, OMA's co-owner and chief architect, Norra Tornen is more than just a pair of high-rise buildings. The thoughtful design embraces Stockholm's unique light and landscape, with protruding window sections and recessed terraces creating a dynamic façade. These features not only add depth but evoke the charm of villa gardens, redefining the traditional concept of city balconies.

Skogskyrkogården

Sockenvägen
Stockholm

@skogskyrkogardenstockholm
skogskyrkogarden.stockholm
+46 8 5083 1730

Skogskyrkogården is a masterpiece where architecture and nature merge. Designed by visionary architects Gunnar Asplund and Sigurd Lewerentz between 1915 and 1940, this UNESCO World Heritage site in southern Stockholm embodies the shift from Nordic Classicism to the clean lines of functionalism. It's a place where the landscape itself tells a story of life, death, and everything in between.

Walking through Skogskyrkogården is like moving through different worlds. The architects intentionally designed the space to blend into its natural surroundings, forests of pine trees, open grasslands, and a gently rolling hill lined with elms. Every architectural feature is placed with purpose, from the solemn granite cross to the Resurrection Chapel, designed by Asplund himself. The true magic of Skogskyrkogården lies in the way it fuses art epochs and architectural styles, creating a deeply personal interpretation of the cycle of life.

Sven-Harrys Konstmuseum

Eastmansvägen 10
11361 Stockholm

@svenharryskonstmuseum
sven-harrys.se
+46 8 5116 0060

Sven-Harrys Konstmuseum, designed by Gert Wingårdh and Anna Höglund, is an stunning building with a gleaming brass façade, situated beside Vasaparken. Opened in 2011, the museum features a 400-square-metre gallery spanning three spacious halls and houses Sven-Harry's private art collection in a replica of his 18th-century manor, Ekholmsnäs, located on the roof terrace. This unique setting offers beautiful views of Vasastan and an intimate glimpse into one of Sweden's largest private collections of Nordic art.

The collection highlights works by Carl Fredrik Hill, Ernst Josephson, August Strindberg, and Helene Schjerfbeck, complemented by furniture from Gio Ponti and Georg Haupt and textiles by Märta Måås-Fjetterström. The museum also includes a restaurant, a shop, and rental apartments.

Tensta
RAMIRENT
RAMIRENT

Tensta Konsthall

Taxingegränd 10
163 04 Spånga

@tenstakonsthall
tenstakonsthall.se
+46 8 360763

If you're looking for contemporary art with a twist, Tensta Konsthall is the spot. Located in the Tensta suburb, the artistic experience starts right when you step off the subway with Helga Henschen's installation A Rose to Immigrants, a poetic tribute to diversity, featuring works from people around the world. Founded in 1998 as a grassroots initiative, Tensta Konsthall has grown into a powerhouse for both local and international contemporary art. The gallery works closely with other independent art spaces in Stockholm, like Konsthall C and Marabouparken, creating a true network for the city's art scene.

Tensta Konsthall's reputation for showcasing groundbreaking work is well-earned. Many artists have had their breakthrough exhibitions here before catching the attention of major international galleries.

Whether you're here for the art or just to enjoy the café, this gallery offers a glimpse into Stockholm's vibrant, multicultural art world.

Tensta konsthall

Index

34 Ettresex / Jade (p. 127)
35 Dusty Deco (p. 131)
36 Grandpa (p. 135)
37 Sneakersnstuff (p. 137)
38 Stora Skuggan (p. 141)
39 Tambur (p. 145)
40 Flattered (p. 149)
41 Svenskt Tenn (p. 153)
42 Östermalms Saluhall (p. 155)
43 Artipelag (p. 161)
44 Carl Eldhs Ateljémuseum (p. 165)
45 ArkDes (p. 169)
46 Fotografiska (p. 173)
47 Liljevalchs (p. 175)
48 Museum of Spirits (p. 179)
49 Norra Tornen (p. 183)
50 Skogskyrkogården (p. 185)
51 Sven-Harrys Konstmuseum (p. 187)
52 Tensta Konsthall (p. 189)

Mads Arlien-Søborg is a Copenhagen-based journalist and lifestyle expert. He holds a master's degree in modern Culture and Communication from University of Copenhagen. Mads has worked with design, fashion and lifestyles for many years. He has hosted several television shows about travel, design and architecture.

New Mags is more than a bookstore; it's a destination where art and literature converge, offering a select array of lifestyle books, magazines, and accessories. Founded in 2016 in Horsens, Jutland by Jesper Svangård and Jesper Oxholm Mikkelsen. Their dream of a space that not only stores but celebrates books culminated in the opening of their first showroom in Copenhagen in 2021.

NOTES

NOTES

NOTES

NOTES

FRONT COVER:
@helmutsdotter

DESTINATION:
© Mads Arlien-Søborg, Mikael-Hornlund, Miladinho, Ru Kal

NEIGHBOURHOODS:
© Mads Arlien-Søborg, Oskar Scheller (Slakthusområdet), Alexander Zvir (Norrmalm), Bram Kloos (Djurgården), @helmutsdotter (Skeppsholmen), Erik G Svensson, stockholmmediabank, Visitstockholm

STAY:
Bank Hotel: © Jens Bergstrand, Joakim Ström, Johannes Maxweller
Berns Hotel: © Johan Nilsson, Mathias Nordgren, Niklas Nyman
Ett Hem: © Magnus Mårding
Hobo: Courtesy of Hobo
Hotel At Six: Courtesy of Hotel At Six
Hotel Skeppsholmen: © Jesper Wikström, Louise Ljunggren, © Lena Larsson
Villa Dahlia: © Magnus Mårding
Nobis Hotel Stockholm: © Beatrice Graalheim
Stockholm Stadshotell: © Henrik Lundell, Erik Olsson

EAT:
Alba Vinbar: Courtesy of Alba Vinbar
Bambi: Courtesy of Bambi
Bar Europa: © Casper Schaber
Bar Montan: © Johan Dehlin
Bleck: © Marcus Lindström
Brutalisten: Courtesy of Brutalisten
Café Nizza: Courtesy of Café Nizza
Drop Coffee: © Christian Gustavsson
Gaia Matbar: Courtesy of Gaia Matbar
Kouthoofd Familie Winkel: © Noah Constantinou
Lillebrors Bageri: Courtesy of Lillebrors Bageri
Persona: © Lefvander
Kvarnen: © Staffan Eliasson
Nationalmuseum: © Erik Lefvander, Pia Ulin
Riche Fenix: Courtesy of Riche Fenix
Savant Bar: © Frances Marais
Solen: © Malin Fränberg, Pierre Björk
Stora Bageriet: Courtesy of Riche Fenix
Svarta Hästens: © Peter Fredriksson

SHOP:
A Days March: © Mikael Lundblad
Acne Studios: © Mikael Olsson
All Blues: © Mikael Olsson
Dusty Deco: © Pierre Björk
Ettresex / Jade: © Sebastian Höglund, @besssan
Grandpa: Courtesy of Grandpa
Konst-ig: © Malte Frey
Sneakersnstuff: Courtesy of Sneakersnstuff
Stora Skuggan: © Mikael Lundblad
Svenskt Tenn: © Pia Ulin
Tambur: © Jenny Forsberg
Flattered: © Erik Lefvander
Östermalm Saluhall: © Åke E:son Lindman

EXPLORE:
ArkDes: © Marco Cappelletti
Artipelag: Courtesy of Artipelag
Carl Eldh Museum: © Nikodem Calczynski
Fotografiska: © Kajsa Göransson, Erik G Svensson
Liljevalch: © Mattias Lindbäck
Museum of Spirits: © Stefan Vettainen
Norra Tornen: © Ossip van Duivenbode, Laurian Ghinitoiu, Norra Tornen Oma Press
Skogskyrkagården: © Alexander Assal
Sven-Harrys Konstmuseum: © Tord-Rikard Söderström
Tensta Konsthall: © Jean-Baptiste Béranger

NEW MAGS CITY GUIDE
STOCKHOLM

Editor-In-Chief: Mads Arlien-Søborg
Publisher: New Mags
Sales: Jesper Svangård, New Mags

Art Direction: Studio8585
Design Director: Mario Depicolzuane
Design & Layout: Benja Pavlin, Varshini KVSS

ISBN: 978-87-94190-73-2

MIX
Paper | Supporting responsible forestry
FSC® C129413

2nd Edition 2026
Printed at Print Best, Estonia, 2026

Published in 2026 by New Mags
& Helmin Publishing

New Mags, Office & Distribution
Vejlevej 13, 8700 Horsens, Denmark
new-mags.com

NEW MAGS

Helmin Publishing
Nivå Strandpark 21, 1
2990 Nivå, Denmark
www.helminpublishing.dk

This book contains a curated selection of the editor's favourite places and should be used for its intended purpose, as a guide. It is by no means comprehensive of all the amazing locations the city has to offer. Since changes may have occurred since publication, we recommend using the contact information for each location to ensure up-to-date details.

The editor and publisher wish to express their gratitude to everyone who played a role in making this book possible: the staff, friends and families, brands, and organizations. A big thank you to Fujifilm® for giving us the opportunity to create beautiful city images for the book.